25 Prophets Book Summary

Arief Muinnudin

Published by Arief Muinnudin, 2024.

While every precaution has been taken in the preparation of this book, the publisher assumes no responsibility for errors or omissions, or for damages resulting from the use of the information contained herein.

25 PROPHETS BOOK SUMMARY

First edition. May 26, 2024.

ISBN: 979-8224421572

Written by Arief Muinnudin.

Table of Contents

1.The Story of Prophet Adam (Ādam)

Introduction

Prophet Adam (Ādam), considered the first human being and prophet in Islamic tradition, holds a significant place in the Quran and Hadith. His story provides foundational lessons on the origins of humanity, the importance of obedience to Allah (God), and the consequences of disobedience. The narrative of Adam encompasses his creation, the divine command to the angels, the rebellion of Iblis (Satan), Adam's life in paradise, the temptation and fall, repentance, and life on Earth.

Creation of Adam

According to Islamic belief, Allah created Adam from clay or dust, making him the first human being. This creation marked a significant event, as Allah intended for Adam to be His vicegerent (Khalifah) on Earth. The Quran describes this event:

"And when your Lord said to the angels, 'Indeed, I will make upon the earth a successive authority.' They said, 'Will You place upon it one who causes corruption therein and sheds blood, while we declare Your praise and sanctify You?' He said, 'Indeed, I know that which you do not know.'" (Quran 2:30)

The Command to the Angels

Upon creating Adam, Allah commanded all the angels to bow down to him in recognition of his unique status and the special knowledge bestowed upon him. All the angels obeyed except Iblis, who was not an angel but a jinn, created from smokeless fire. Iblis refused out of arrogance and pride, stating that he was superior to Adam.

"And [mention] when We said to the angels, 'Prostrate before Adam'; so they prostrated, except for Iblis. He refused and was arrogant and became of the disbelievers." (Quran 2:34)

The Rebellion of Iblis

Iblis's refusal to bow down to Adam led to his expulsion from paradise and his transformation into Satan (Shaytan). He vowed to lead Adam and his descendants astray to prove their unworthiness. Allah granted Iblis respite until the Day of Judgment but warned that he would have no power over His true servants.

"He said, 'My Lord, because You have put me in error, I will surely make [disobedience] attractive to them on earth, and I will mislead them all. Except, among them, Your chosen servants.'" (Quran 15:39-40)

Life in Paradise

Adam was placed in paradise, a place of peace and abundance. Allah created a companion for Adam, Hawwa (Eve), from his rib to provide him with company and support. Adam and Hawwa lived happily in paradise with only one prohibition: they were not to eat from a specific tree.

"And We said, 'O Adam, dwell, you and your wife, in Paradise and eat therefrom in [ease and] abundance from wherever you will. But do not approach this tree, lest you be among the wrongdoers.'" (Quran 2:35)

The Temptation and Fall

Iblis, seeking revenge, tempted Adam and Hawwa to eat from the forbidden tree by promising them immortality and a kingdom that would never deteriorate. Despite their initial resistance, they eventually succumbed to Iblis's whispers and ate from the tree. This act of disobedience led to their immediate realization of their error and their exposure, symbolized by their nakedness.

"But Satan whispered to them to make apparent to them that which was concealed from them of their private parts. He said, 'Your Lord did not forbid you this tree except that you become angels or become of the immortal.'" (Quran 7:20)

Repentance and Forgiveness

Realizing their mistake, Adam and Hawwa turned to Allah in sincere repentance. Allah, in His infinite mercy, accepted their repentance and forgave them. However, as a consequence of their disobedience, they were sent down to Earth to live and fulfill their role as Allah's vicegerents.

"Then Adam received from his Lord [some] words, and He accepted his repentance. Indeed, it is He who is the Accepting of repentance, the Merciful." (Quran 2:37)

Life on Earth

Adam and Hawwa began their life on Earth, striving to fulfill their duties and responsibilities. They were blessed with children and became the progenitors of the human race. Adam served as the first prophet, guiding his descendants to worship Allah and live righteous lives. His story serves as a reminder of the importance of obedience to Allah, the consequences of disobedience, and the boundless mercy and forgiveness of the Creator.

Legacy

Prophet Adam's legacy is profound, as he is considered the father of humanity and the first to receive divine guidance. His story teaches lessons about humility, repentance, and the eternal struggle between good and evil. Adam's life exemplifies the human experience of trial, error, repentance, and redemption, serving as a guiding narrative for all his descendants.

Conclusion

The story of Prophet Adam in Islam encapsulates the beginning of human existence and the essence of the relationship between humanity and the divine. It underscores the themes of creation, temptation, fall, repentance, and divine mercy, offering timeless lessons for believers. Through Adam's story, Muslims are reminded of their purpose on Earth, the importance of obedience to Allah, and the hope of forgiveness through sincere repentance.

2.The Story of Prophet Idris (Enoch)

Introduction

Prophet Idris (Enoch) holds a revered place in Islamic tradition as a prophet of guidance and wisdom. His story, although brief in the Quran, carries profound lessons about faith, righteousness, and the pursuit of knowledge. Idris is mentioned as a prophet who lived during a time of great challenges and who remained steadfast in his devotion to Allah.

Early Life and Prophethood

Idris was born in Babylon and is believed to be a descendant of Prophet Seth, the son of Adam. He grew up in a society marked by idolatry and moral decay. Despite these challenges, Idris remained devoted to Allah and sought knowledge and wisdom. Allah bestowed prophethood upon him, making him a beacon of guidance for his people.

Preaching and Guidance

As a prophet, Idris called his people to monotheism (Tawhid) and righteousness. He urged them to turn away from idol worship and to follow the path of virtue and piety. Idris's teachings emphasized the importance of faith, moral integrity, and seeking knowledge as a means of drawing closer to Allah.

The Book of Idris

According to Islamic tradition, Idris received a divine scripture, known as the "Book of Idris" (Sahifah Idris). This scripture contained wisdom, guidance, and laws for his community. While the contents of this book are not detailed in the Quran, it is regarded as a source of divine knowledge and guidance during Idris's time.

Ascension and Legacy

One of the unique aspects of Prophet Idris's story is his ascension to heaven. Islamic tradition holds that Idris was lifted to the heavens without experiencing death, similar to the ascension of Prophet Isa (Jesus). This miraculous event elevated Idris's status as a prophet and exemplified his close relationship with Allah.

Mention in the Quran

The Quran mentions Prophet Idris in a few verses, highlighting his righteousness and elevated status:

"And mention in the Book, Idris. Indeed, he was a man of truth and a prophet. And We raised him to a high station." (Quran 19:56-57)

These verses affirm Idris's truthfulness, prophethood, and elevated spiritual rank.

Conclusion

Prophet Idris's story serves as a reminder of the enduring legacy of faith, wisdom, and devotion to Allah. His steadfastness in a challenging environment, his commitment to spreading divine guidance, and his ascension to heaven symbolize the rewards of piety and righteousness. Idris's story inspires believers to emulate his virtues, seek knowledge, and strive for closeness to Allah.

3.The Story of Prophet Nuh (Noah)

Introduction

Prophet Nuh (Noah) is a central figure in Islamic tradition, known for his unwavering faith, perseverance, and mission to warn his people of impending divine punishment. His story, encompassing the construction of the ark, the flood, and the survival of believers, carries profound lessons about patience, obedience to Allah, and the consequences of disbelief.

Early Life and Calling to Prophethood

Prophet Nuh was born into a society that had deviated from the path of righteousness. Idolatry and moral corruption were rampant, leading people away from the worship of Allah. Despite these challenges, Nuh remained steadfast in his faith from a young age. Allah chose him as a prophet and tasked him with calling his people to monotheism (Tawhid) and righteousness.

The Call to Repentance

Nuh's mission began with sincere and earnest calls to his people, urging them to abandon their idols and return to the worship of the one true God. He warned them of the consequences of their actions and invited them to seek forgiveness and guidance from Allah.

"And We certainly sent Noah to his people, and he said, 'O my people, worship Allah; you have no deity other than Him. Indeed, I fear for you the punishment of a tremendous Day!'" (Quran 7:59)

Despite Nuh's persistent efforts, only a few believed in his message, while the majority rejected him and continued in their disobedience.

The Construction of the Ark

As his people persisted in disbelief and defiance, Nuh received divine guidance to build an ark (ship) as a means of salvation from the impending flood. Following Allah's instructions with unwavering faith, Nuh and his followers diligently constructed the massive ark over many years, facing ridicule and mockery from disbelievers.

The Flood and Salvation

When the appointed time of punishment arrived, Allah commanded Nuh to gather believers and pairs of every species of animal onto the ark. The floodwaters engulfed the land, destroying everything except those on the ark.

"And it was said, 'O earth, swallow your water, and O sky, withhold [your rain].' And the water subsided, and the matter was accomplished, and the ship came to rest on the [mountain of] Judiyy. And it was said, 'Away with the wrongdoing people!'" (Quran 11:44)

The ark became a symbol of divine mercy and salvation, as Nuh and his followers survived the cataclysmic flood through their faith and obedience.

After the Flood

After the floodwaters receded and the land was once again habitable, Nuh and his followers disembarked from the ark. They started afresh, rebuilding their lives and civilization while remaining steadfast in their devotion to Allah.

Legacy and Lessons

Prophet Nuh's story carries timeless lessons for believers. It emphasizes the importance of patience, perseverance, and unwavering faith in the face of adversity. Nuh's commitment to delivering Allah's message, his trust in divine guidance, and the miraculous survival of believers aboard the ark showcase the power of faith and obedience.

Conclusion

Prophet Nuh's story serves as a reminder of the consequences of disbelief, the mercy of Allah, and the rewards of steadfastness in faith. His example inspires believers to remain resolute in their devotion to Allah, to invite others to righteousness, and to trust in divine guidance even in the most challenging times.

4. The Story of Prophet Hud (Eber)

Introduction

Prophet Hud (Eber) is a significant figure in Islamic tradition, known for his mission to guide his people and warn them of the consequences of their disbelief and wrongdoing. His story, recorded in the Quran, highlights themes of patience, steadfastness, and the divine justice of Allah.

Early Life and Background

Prophet Hud lived in ancient Arabia among the 'Ad people, a wealthy and powerful civilization known for their arrogance and idolatry. Despite their material wealth, the 'Ad people had turned away from the worship of Allah and indulged in oppression, pride, and disobedience.

Hud's Prophethood and Mission

Allah chose Hud as a prophet and sent him to his people with a message of monotheism (Tawhid) and righteousness. Hud called upon the 'Ad people to abandon their idols and return to the worship of Allah, warning them of the consequences of their actions if they continued in their disbelief and wrongdoing.

"And to the 'Ad [We sent] their brother Hud. He said, 'O my people, worship Allah; you have no deity other than Him. You are not but inventors [of falsehood].'" (Quran 11:50)

Despite Hud's sincere and earnest calls, the 'Ad people rejected his message and mocked him, blinded by their arrogance and worldly pride.

The Punishment and Destruction

As the 'Ad people persisted in their defiance and disbelief, Allah decreed a severe punishment upon them. A mighty windstorm, unlike any they had experienced before, swept through their lands, destroying everything in its path and leaving them in utter ruin.

"So when Our command came, We saved Hud and those who believed with him, by mercy from Us, and We saved them from a harsh punishment." (Quran 11:58)

Hud and those who believed in him were saved from the punishment by the mercy of Allah, while the 'Ad people faced the consequences of their arrogance and disobedience.

Lessons and Legacy

Prophet Hud's story carries important lessons for believers. It highlights the dangers of arrogance, disbelief, and oppression, as well as the importance of sincere repentance and obedience to Allah. Hud's unwavering commitment to delivering Allah's message, despite facing ridicule and rejection, serves as a model of patience and perseverance in the face of adversity.

Conclusion

Prophet Hud's story serves as a reminder of the consequences of arrogance and disbelief, as well as the mercy and justice of Allah. His mission to guide his people and call them to righteousness underscores the timeless message of monotheism, humility, and submission to the divine will. Hud's legacy continues to inspire believers to uphold the principles of faith, righteousness, and compassion in their lives.

5.The Story of Prophet Saleh (Methusaleh)

Introduction

Prophet Saleh, known as Saleh in Islamic tradition, was sent by Allah to guide the Thamud people, an ancient Arabian civilization. His story, recorded in the Quran, carries profound lessons about monotheism, righteousness, and the consequences of arrogance and disobedience.

Early Life and Background

Saleh was born into the tribe of Thamud, descendants of Prophet Noah (Nuh). The Thamud were known for their advanced civilization and skills in architecture and carving. However, they had strayed from the worship of Allah and engaged in idolatry, oppression, and wickedness.

Prophethood and Mission

Allah chose Saleh as a prophet and sent him to his people with a clear message: worship Allah alone and abandon the worship of idols. Saleh called upon the Thamud to recognize the signs of Allah's existence and power in the creation around them, urging them to repent and follow the path of righteousness.

"And to the Thamud [We sent] their brother Saleh. He said, 'O my people, worship Allah; you have no deity other than Him. He has produced you from the earth and settled you in it, so ask forgiveness of Him and then repent to Him. Indeed, my Lord is near and responsive.'" (Quran 11:61)

Saleh emphasized the importance of seeking forgiveness and turning back to Allah before facing His divine wrath for their disobedience.

The She-Camel Miracle

One of the significant miracles associated with Prophet Saleh is the she-camel (Al-Naqah) that Allah sent as a sign of His power and a test for the Thamud. The she-camel emerged from a rock as a miraculous creation, with specific conditions attached to its presence. The Thamud were commanded not to harm the she-camel and to allow it to drink from the water freely.

"And We sent to Thamud their brother Saleh, saying, 'Worship Allah.' And at once they were two parties conflicting." (Quran 27:45)

Disbelief and Punishment

Despite witnessing the miraculous signs and hearing Saleh's warnings, the Thamud people divided into two groups: those who believed in Saleh's message and those who remained defiant in their disbelief and arrogance. The disbelievers plotted against the she-camel, eventually killing it despite Saleh's warnings.

"And We sent upon them one blast from the sky, and they became like the dry twig fragments of an [animal] pen." (Quran 54:31)

As a consequence of their disbelief, Allah sent a powerful punishment upon the Thamud in the form of a violent earthquake, destroying them and leaving their dwellings in ruins. Only those who believed in Saleh and followed Allah's commandments were saved from the calamity.

Lessons and Legacy

Prophet Saleh's story carries timeless lessons about the importance of monotheism, obedience to Allah, and the consequences of disbelief and arrogance. His unwavering commitment to delivering Allah's message, despite facing opposition and persecution, serves as a model of courage and faith.

Conclusion

Prophet Saleh's story in Islamic tradition highlights the divine justice of Allah and the ultimate fate of those who reject His guidance. It serves as a reminder for believers to remain steadfast in their faith, to uphold righteousness, and to heed the warnings and lessons from the stories of the prophets.

6.The Story of Prophet Lut (Lot)

Introduction

Prophet Lut (Lot) holds a significant place in Islamic tradition as a messenger of Allah sent to guide his people and warn them against immoral behavior. His story, recorded in the Quran, carries profound lessons about the consequences of sin, the importance of righteousness, and the mercy of Allah.

Early Life and Background

Prophet Lut was the nephew of Prophet Ibrahim (Abraham) and lived during a time when the people of Sodom and Gomorrah had deviated from the path of righteousness. They engaged in widespread immorality, including homosexuality, arrogance, and oppression.

Prophethood and Mission

Allah chose Lut as a prophet and sent him to his people with a clear message: abandon their sinful ways, worship Allah alone, and follow the path of righteousness. Lut warned his people of the consequences of their actions and urged them to repent before facing divine punishment.

"And [mention] Lot, when he said to his people, 'Indeed, you commit such immorality as no one has preceded you with from among the worlds. Indeed, you approach men with desire, instead of women. Rather, you are a transgressing people.'" (Quran 7:80-81)

The Challenge and Test

The people of Sodom and Gomorrah rejected Lut's message and persisted in their sinful behavior. They mocked Lut and accused him of being deluded. In response, Lut continued to advise them and sought Allah's guidance and support.

Divine Punishment

Despite Lut's efforts, the people of Sodom and Gomorrah remained defiant. In response to their wickedness, Allah decreed a severe punishment upon them. The Quran describes the punishment as a catastrophic event, possibly a combination of natural disasters like earthquakes and a rain of stones.

"So We saved him and his family, except for his wife; We destined her to be of those who remained behind. And We rained upon them a rain [of stones], and evil was the rain of those who were warned." (Quran 26:170-173)

Salvation of Prophet Lut

Before the punishment befell his people, Allah instructed Lut to leave the city with his family, except for his wife, who chose to remain with the disbelievers. Lut and his believing family members were saved from the destruction, underscoring the importance of faith and obedience.

Lessons and Legacy

Prophet Lut's story carries timeless lessons about the consequences of immorality, the importance of standing up for righteousness, and the mercy of Allah. It serves as a warning against sinful behavior and emphasizes the need for repentance and obedience to Allah's commandments.

Conclusion

Prophet Lut's story in Islamic tradition highlights the divine justice of Allah and the ultimate fate of those who persist in disobedience. It serves as a reminder for believers to uphold moral values, to reject sinful behavior, and to seek forgiveness and guidance from Allah.

7.The Story of Prophet Ibrahim (Abraham)

Introduction

Prophet Ibrahim (Abraham) holds a revered position in Islamic tradition as a prominent prophet and patriarch. His story, deeply woven into the fabric of monotheism, faith, and devotion to Allah, carries profound lessons for believers.

Early Life and Calling to Prophethood

Prophet Ibrahim was born into a family that practiced idolatry, but from a young age, he questioned the worship of idols and sought the truth. Allah blessed Ibrahim with wisdom and guidance, leading him to recognize the oneness of God (Tawhid) amidst a society steeped in polytheism.

The Monotheistic Message

As Ibrahim matured, his conviction in monotheism strengthened, and he began to openly call people to worship Allah alone, rejecting the worship of idols and false deities. His message emphasized the purity of faith, submission to Allah's will, and the importance of righteousness.

"And [mention] when Abraham said to his father and his people, 'Indeed, I am disassociated from what you worship except for He who created me; and indeed, He will guide me.'" (Quran 43:26-27)

The Tests of Faith

Allah tested Ibrahim's faith and devotion through a series of trials known as the "Kashf al-Ibtillat" or the Unveiling of Trials. These trials included Ibrahim's confrontation with his father and people, his survival from the

"

fire, his migration, the command to sacrifice his son, and the rebuilding of the Kaaba.

Confrontation with Idolatry

Ibrahim's rejection of idol worship led to conflict with his father and community. Despite their opposition, Ibrahim remained steadfast in his belief in the oneness of Allah.

Survival from the Fire

The most famous trial is Ibrahim's survival from a massive fire set by his people to punish him for his beliefs. Allah commanded the fire to be cool and peaceful for Ibrahim, demonstrating divine protection and support for His devoted servant.

Migration and Establishing Faith

Ibrahim migrated with his family, including his wife Hajar (Hagar) and son Isma'il (Ishmael), to a barren land that would later become known as Makkah (Mecca). There, he established the foundations of monotheism and laid the cornerstone of the Kaaba, a symbol of worship and unity for generations to come.

Sacrifice of His Son

One of the most profound tests of Ibrahim's faith was when Allah commanded him to sacrifice his beloved son, Isma'il. Despite the immense emotional turmoil, Ibrahim remained obedient to Allah's command. As Ibrahim prepared to sacrifice Isma'il, Allah replaced him with a ram, symbolizing the ultimate submission to Allah's will.

"And We ransomed him with a great sacrifice." (Quran 37:107)

Legacy and Blessings

Prophet Ibrahim's unwavering faith, devotion, and obedience earned him the title "Khalilullah," the Friend of Allah. His story serves as a beacon of guidance for believers, highlighting the virtues of trust, patience, and submission to the divine will.

Conclusion

Prophet Ibrahim's story in Islamic tradition encapsulates the essence of monotheism, devotion, and sacrifice for the sake of Allah. His life serves as a timeless example of faith and righteousness, inspiring believers to emulate his unwavering commitment to Allah and His commandments.

8. The Story of Prophet Isma'il (Ishmael)

Introduction

Prophet Isma'il (Ishmael) is an important figure in Islamic tradition, known for his lineage as the son of Prophet Ibrahim (Abraham) and his significant role in the construction of the Kaaba in Makkah. His story embodies themes of faith, sacrifice, and divine blessings.

Birth and Early Life

Isma'il was born to Prophet Ibrahim and his wife Hajar (Hagar) in response to Ibrahim's supplication for progeny. His birth brought immense joy to his parents, who cherished him deeply.

Settlement in Makkah

Prophet Ibrahim was commanded by Allah to take Hajar and Isma'il to a barren valley near the ancient city of Makkah (Mecca) and leave them there. This event is known as the "Mawqif al-Wida'" or the Standing Place of Farewell.

"And [mention] when Abraham said, 'My Lord, make this city [Makkah] secure and keep me and my sons away from worshipping idols.'" (Quran 14:35)

Ibrahim's supplication reflected his desire for a pure and monotheistic environment for his family.

The Well of Zamzam

As Hajar and Isma'il were left in the barren valley, they faced hardship due to the lack of water. In her search for water, Hajar ran between the hills of Safa and Marwa seven times, seeking help and praying to Allah for relief. Allah responded to her supplication by causing the miraculous spring of Zamzam to gush forth near Isma'il.

"And We made the son of Mary and his mother a sign and sheltered them within a high ground having level [areas] and flowing water." (Quran 23:50)

The well of Zamzam became a source of sustenance and blessing for Isma'il and his mother, providing water for generations to come.

The Building of the Kaaba

Prophet Ibrahim received a command from Allah to rebuild the Kaaba, the sacred house of worship originally constructed by Prophet Adam. Ibrahim and Isma'il worked together to raise the foundations of the Kaaba, following divine guidance.

"And [mention] when Abraham was raising the foundations of the House and [with him] Isma'il, [saying], 'Our Lord, accept [this] from us. Indeed, You are the Hearing, the Knowing.'" (Quran 2:127)

Their devotion and submission to Allah's command exemplified the importance of faith and obedience.

Legacy and Blessings

Prophet Isma'il's lineage continued through his descendants, including the Prophet Muhammad (peace be upon him), who was from the Quraysh tribe descended from Isma'il. The well of Zamzam and the Kaaba remain symbols of divine blessings and unity for Muslims worldwide.

Conclusion

Prophet Isma'il's story in Islamic tradition highlights the significance of faith, perseverance, and divine providence. His role in the construction of the Kaaba and the establishment of the sacred city of Makkah symbolize the eternal blessings bestowed upon the righteous and the fulfillment of Allah's promises to His devoted servants.

9.The Story of Prophet Ishaq (Isaac)

Introduction

Prophet Ishaq (Isaac) is a revered figure in Islamic tradition, known for his lineage as the son of Prophet Ibrahim (Abraham) and his significant role in the propagation of monotheism. His story, recorded in the Quran, carries profound lessons about faith, trust in Allah, and the fulfillment of divine promises.

Birth and Early Life

Prophet Ishaq was born to Prophet Ibrahim and his wife Sarah (Sara), who had been barren for many years until Allah blessed them with Ishaq in their old age. His birth was a testament to the miraculous power of Allah and a fulfillment of Ibrahim's prayers for offspring.

Covenant and Prophethood

Ishaq grew up in an environment of faith and devotion to Allah, inheriting the legacy of monotheism from his father Ibrahim. Allah bestowed prophethood upon Ishaq, continuing the divine message of monotheism and righteousness.

Family and Descendants

Prophet Ishaq married Rebekah (Rifqah), and they were blessed with twin sons, Esau (Esav) and Jacob (Yaqub). Jacob later became a prophet and was known for his piety and devotion to Allah.

Trust in Allah's Promises

One of the significant events in Ishaq's life was the test of sacrifice, similar to the one faced by his father Ibrahim. Allah tested Ishaq's faith by commanding him to sacrifice his son, Jacob. However, before Ishaq could carry out the sacrifice, Allah replaced Jacob with a ram, demonstrating divine mercy and the fulfillment of His promises.

Legacy and Blessings

Prophet Ishaq's lineage continued through his descendants, who played pivotal roles in the propagation of monotheism and the establishment of righteous communities. His story emphasizes the importance of faith, obedience to Allah, and trust in divine promises.

Conclusion

Prophet Ishaq's story in Islamic tradition highlights the continuity of prophethood and monotheism within the lineage of Ibrahim's family. His role as a prophet and the fulfillment of divine promises underscore the timeless principles of faith, devotion, and reliance on Allah's guidance.

10.The Story of Prophet Ya'qub (Jacob)

Introduction

Prophet Ya'qub (Jacob) is a significant figure in Islamic tradition, known for his righteousness, piety, and role as a prophet in the lineage of Ibrahim (Abraham). His story, recorded in the Quran, carries profound lessons about patience, faith, and the importance of maintaining moral integrity in the face of adversity.

Early Life and Family

Prophet Ya'qub was the son of Prophet Ishaq (Isaac) and the grandson of Prophet Ibrahim (Abraham). He grew up in a household of faith and devotion to Allah, inheriting the legacy of prophethood from his ancestors.

Covenant and Prophethood

Allah bestowed prophethood upon Ya'qub, continuing the divine message of monotheism and righteousness passed down through generations. Ya'qub was known for his wisdom, piety, and commitment to guiding his people toward the path of righteousness.

The Twelve Sons

One of the significant aspects of Ya'qub's life was his twelve sons, who became the progenitors of the twelve tribes of Israel (Bani Israel). Each son had distinct characteristics and roles, contributing to the development of the righteous community guided by Ya'qub's teachings.

Joseph (Yusuf) and the Coat of Many Colors

One of the most famous narratives associated with Prophet Ya'qub is the story of his son Joseph (Yusuf). Ya'qub's deep love for Joseph was evident, symbolized by the gift of a coat of many colors. This love led to jealousy and resentment among Joseph's brothers, who conspired to harm him.

Patience and Faith

Despite facing challenges, including the betrayal and disappearance of Joseph, Ya'qub remained patient and steadfast in his faith. His unwavering trust in Allah's wisdom and divine plan exemplified the importance of patience and reliance on Allah during difficult times.

Reunion and Forgiveness

After years of separation, Ya'qub was reunited with Joseph, who had risen to a position of authority in Egypt. The reunion and reconciliation with his sons marked a period of forgiveness, mercy, and divine blessings.

Legacy and Lessons

Prophet Ya'qub's story in Islamic tradition highlights the virtues of patience, forgiveness, and maintaining faith during trials. His role as a prophet and leader of the righteous community serves as a model for believers, emphasizing the importance of upholding moral values and seeking Allah's guidance in all aspects of life.

Conclusion

Prophet Ya'qub's story in Islamic tradition underscores the enduring principles of faith, righteousness, and family unity. His life serves as a timeless example of perseverance, trust in Allah, and the rewards of maintaining moral integrity, even in the face of adversity.

11. The Story of Prophet Yusuf (Joseph)

Introduction

The story of Prophet Yusuf (Joseph) is one of the most captivating and detailed narratives in the Quran, showcasing themes of resilience, faith, patience, and divine wisdom. It spans from his early life as a beloved son to his rise to prominence in Egypt and eventual reunion with his family.

Childhood and Dreams

Prophet Yusuf was the son of Prophet Ya'qub (Jacob) and grew up in a family of prophethood and righteousness. He was known for his exceptional beauty and noble character. At a young age, Yusuf experienced vivid dreams that foretold his future greatness, symbolized by celestial bodies bowing down to him.

Betrayal and Enslavement

Yusuf's brothers, overcome by jealousy, plotted to harm him and threw him into a well, intending to rid themselves of his perceived favoritism. He was then sold into slavery in Egypt, where he caught the attention of a high-ranking official named Potiphar, who took him into his household.

Trial and Temptation

In Potiphar's household, Yusuf faced trials and temptations when approached by Potiphar's wife with immoral advances. Despite the allure and pressure, Yusuf remained steadfast in his faith and integrity, refusing to betray his principles.

Imprisonment and Interpretation of Dreams

As a result of false accusations, Yusuf was unjustly thrown into prison. However, even in prison, his reputation for interpreting dreams reached the ears of fellow inmates. Yusuf's ability to interpret dreams accurately, as inspired by Allah, earned him favor and respect among prisoners and officials alike.

Rise to Power

Yusuf's talent in interpreting dreams caught the attention of the king of Egypt, who sought his expertise. Yusuf correctly interpreted the king's dream about seven years of abundance followed by seven years of famine. Impressed by Yusuf's wisdom, the king appointed him as a high-ranking official in charge of managing the country's resources during the famine.

Reunion with Family

During the famine, Yusuf's brothers traveled to Egypt seeking provisions. Unaware of Yusuf's true identity, they came before him seeking assistance. Yusuf recognized them but kept his identity hidden initially, testing their remorse and sincerity. Eventually, Yusuf revealed himself to his brothers, and they were reunited tearfully.

Forgiveness and Reconciliation

Despite the past betrayals and hardships, Yusuf forgave his brothers, emphasizing that Allah had turned their adversity into a blessing by reuniting them and granting them repentance. The family, including Prophet Ya'qub, was reunited in Egypt, and Yusuf's position and wisdom brought honor and prosperity to his family and the land.

Lessons and Legacy

The story of Prophet Yusuf carries profound lessons about resilience in the face of adversity, the importance of maintaining faith and integrity, and the ultimate reward of forgiveness and reconciliation. It showcases

Allah's wisdom in orchestrating events for the greater good and highlights the power of patience and trust in divine plans.

Conclusion

Prophet Yusuf's story is a testament to the transformative power of faith, perseverance, and forgiveness. His journey from hardship to triumph serves as a timeless inspiration for believers, reminding them of the enduring virtues that lead to Allah's blessings and mercy.

12.The Story of Prophet Shu'aib (Jethro)

Introduction

Prophet Shu'aib (Jethro) is a respected figure in Islamic tradition, known for his wisdom, integrity, and role as a prophet sent to guide his people. His story, mentioned in the Quran, highlights themes of justice, ethical conduct, and the consequences of corruption and oppression.

Background and Community

Prophet Shu'aib was sent to the people of Madyan, an ancient Arab tribe known for their unethical practices, dishonesty in trade, and exploitation of others. Their society was marked by corruption, greed, and a lack of moral values.

Prophethood and Mission

Allah chose Shu'aib as a prophet and sent him to his people with a clear message: uphold justice, honesty in dealings, and worship Allah alone. Shu'aib called upon the people of Madyan to abandon their corrupt ways, treat others fairly, and fulfill their obligations to Allah.

"And to Madyan [We sent] their brother Shu'aib. He said, 'O my people, worship Allah; you have no deity other than Him. And do not decrease from the measure and the scale. Indeed, I see you in prosperity, but indeed, I fear for you the punishment of an all-encompassing Day.'" (Quran 11:84-85)

Opposition and Resilience

Despite Shu'aib's sincere calls and warnings, the people of Madyan rejected his message and continued their unjust practices. They mocked Shu'aib and accused him of being a troublemaker.

The She-Camel Miracle

Similar to the miracle of the she-camel sent to Prophet Saleh's people, Allah provided a sign to the people of Madyan in the form of a miraculous she-camel. Shu'aib warned the people not to harm the she-camel and to allow it to drink from the water freely as a test of their obedience to Allah's commandments.

Divine Punishment

The people of Madyan, blinded by their arrogance and defiance, conspired to kill the she-camel, disregarding Shu'aib's warnings. As a consequence of their disbelief and wrongdoing, Allah sent a severe punishment upon them, destroying their community and leaving them in ruin.

"And We sent upon them the floodgate1 and locusts and lice and frogs and blood as distinct signs, but they were arrogant and were a criminal people." (Quran 7:133)

Legacy and Lessons

Prophet Shu'aib's story in Islamic tradition serves as a reminder of the importance of ethical conduct, justice, and obedience to Allah's commandments. His unwavering commitment to upholding moral values and guiding his people despite adversity highlights the virtues of resilience and steadfastness in faith.

Conclusion

Prophet Shu'aib's story underscores the consequences of corruption, oppression, and arrogance, as well as the importance of righteousness and ethical behavior. His role as a prophet and reformer exemplifies the timeless principles of justice, integrity, and devotion to Allah's guidance.

13.The Story of Prophet Ayyub (Job)

Introduction

Prophet Ayyub (Job) is a revered figure in Islamic tradition, known for his patience, perseverance, and unwavering faith in Allah during times of severe trials and tribulations. His story, mentioned in the Quran, serves as a profound lesson in resilience, trust in Allah, and the ultimate reward of steadfastness.

Righteousness and Blessings

Prophet Ayyub was a pious and wealthy man, blessed with abundant wealth, a loving family, and good health. He was known for his devotion to Allah, gratitude for blessings, and generosity towards others.

Trials and Afflictions

Allah tested Ayyub's faith and patience by allowing severe trials to befall him. He lost his wealth, his children, and was afflicted with a debilitating illness that caused immense suffering and hardship.

Steadfastness and Supplication

Despite his overwhelming trials, Ayyub remained steadfast in his faith and continued to worship and supplicate to Allah. He never wavered in his belief in Allah's mercy and wisdom, maintaining patience and trust in divine plans.

The Test of Family and Friends

Ayyub's wife and friends initially questioned his patience and faith, urging him to seek relief or curse Allah. However, Ayyub remained steadfast, responding with patience and trust in Allah's decree.

"And We found him patient, an excellent servant. Indeed, he was one repeatedly turning back [to Allah]." (Quran 38:44)

Restoration and Blessings

As a reward for his unwavering patience and faith, Allah blessed Ayyub with complete healing from his illness, restored his wealth and family, and bestowed upon him even greater blessings than before.

"And We restored his family to him, and the like thereof with them, as a mercy from Us and a reminder for the worshippers [of Allah]." (Quran 38:43)

Lessons and Legacy

Prophet Ayyub's story in Islamic tradition serves as a powerful example of patience, perseverance, and trust in Allah during times of adversity. His unwavering faith and resilience in the face of severe trials inspire believers to maintain steadfastness and reliance on Allah's mercy and wisdom.

Conclusion

Prophet Ayyub's story highlights the transformative power of patience, faith, and devotion to Allah. His exemplary life serves as a timeless lesson in trusting Allah's plans, remaining patient during hardships, and experiencing the ultimate reward of divine blessings and mercy.

14. The Story of Prophet Dhul-Kifl (Ezekiel)

Introduction

Prophet Dhul-Kifl, also known as Ezekiel in some traditions, is a figure mentioned briefly in Islamic sources, primarily in the Quran. While his story is not as extensively detailed as other prophets, there are some aspects known about him that are worth mentioning.

Mention in the Quran

Dhul-Kifl is mentioned twice in the Quran, in Surah Al-Anbiya (Chapter 21) and Surah Sad (Chapter 38). However, the Quran does not provide extensive details about his life or prophetic mission.

Identity and Background

The identity of Dhul-Kifl is subject to interpretation, with various opinions among scholars. Some identify him as Ezekiel, a biblical prophet, while others suggest he may be a different figure from the Middle Eastern region.

Virtuous Qualities

The Quran describes Dhul-Kifl as a righteous and patient servant of Allah. His mention in the Quran serves as a reminder of the diversity of prophets and the universality of prophethood across different communities.

Interpretations and Narrations

Islamic tradition does not provide elaborate narratives or stories specific to Dhul-Kifl's life or teachings. Instead, his mention in the Quran is often used to emphasize the continuity of prophethood and the importance of righteousness and patience in serving Allah.

Lessons and Legacy

While Dhul-Kifl's story is relatively limited in Islamic sources, his mention in the Quran underscores the diversity of prophets and the universal message of monotheism, righteousness, and devotion to Allah. Believers are encouraged to reflect on the virtues attributed to Dhul-Kifl and to emulate his qualities of piety and patience in their own lives.

Conclusion

Prophet Dhul-Kifl's brief mention in Islamic tradition serves as a reminder of the diverse array of prophets sent by Allah throughout history. While specific details about his life and mission are not extensively elaborated upon, his inclusion in the Quran emphasizes the overarching message of monotheism, righteousness, and steadfastness in faith.

15.The Story of Prophet Musa (Moses)

Introduction

The story of Prophet Musa (Moses) is one of the most detailed and significant narratives in Islamic tradition, occupying a central place in the Quran and serving as a profound example of courage, faith, leadership, and the power of divine intervention. Here is a comprehensive account of his life and mission:

Early Life and Background

Prophet Musa was born into the Israelites during a time when the Pharaoh of Egypt oppressed and enslaved them. His birth coincided with a decree by the Pharaoh to kill all newborn Israelite males, fearing a prophecy of a child who would challenge his authority.

Divine Protection and Adoption

To protect Musa from the Pharaoh's decree, his mother placed him in a basket and set him afloat on the river Nile. Allah guided the basket to reach the Pharaoh's palace, where Musa was discovered and adopted by the Pharaoh's wife, Asiya bint Muzahim. Thus, Musa grew up in the palace under royal protection.

Call to Prophethood

As Musa matured, Allah chose him as a prophet and tasked him with the mission of guiding the Israelites out of bondage and oppression in Egypt. Musa was granted miraculous abilities, including the staff that transformed into a serpent and his hand that radiated with divine light.

Confrontation with Pharaoh

When Musa reached adulthood, he confronted the Pharaoh, demanding the freedom of the Israelites and the cessation of their oppression. Musa's miracles, including the parting of the sea (the miracle of the Red Sea), demonstrated Allah's power and authority.

Exodus and Miracles

Through a series of miracles and trials, including the plagues upon Egypt, Musa led the Israelites in their exodus from Egypt, crossing the Red Sea miraculously as the waters parted to allow safe passage. This event symbolized divine intervention and the liberation of the oppressed.

Revelation of the Torah

During the journey, Musa received divine revelations, including the Torah (Tawrat), which contained guidance and laws for the Israelites to follow. The Torah emphasized monotheism, ethical conduct, and justice.

Forty Years in the Wilderness

The Israelites wandered in the wilderness for forty years as a test of their faith and obedience to Allah. Musa provided leadership, guidance, and teachings during this period, ensuring the spiritual and moral development of his people.

Legacy and Impact

Prophet Musa's leadership, courage, and unwavering faith left a lasting legacy in Islamic tradition. His story is a testament to the power of perseverance, the importance of standing up against oppression, and the rewards of steadfastness in faith.

Conclusion

The story of Prophet Musa in Islamic tradition serves as a timeless inspiration for believers, emphasizing the virtues of courage, faith, leadership, and the transformative impact of divine intervention. Musa's life and mission continue to resonate as a symbol of hope, justice, and the ultimate triumph of truth over falsehood.

16.The Story of Prophet Harun (Aaron)

Introduction

Prophet Harun (Aaron) is a significant figure in Islamic tradition, known for his role as a prophet, advisor, and supporter of his brother, Prophet Musa (Moses). His story, intertwined with Musa's mission and the liberation of the Israelites, showcases themes of loyalty, leadership, and the importance of unity in faith.

Early Life and Family

Harun was born into the lineage of the Israelites during a time of oppression and slavery in Egypt under the rule of the Pharaoh. He was the older brother of Prophet Musa and played a crucial role in their shared mission to guide their people and confront the Pharaoh.

Appointment as Prophet

Allah appointed Harun as a prophet alongside Musa, granting him wisdom, eloquence, and the ability to support Musa in his mission. Harun's role as a prophet was to aid Musa in conveying Allah's message to the Israelites and to provide guidance and leadership.

Support for Musa

Harun supported Musa throughout their mission, standing by him during confrontations with the Pharaoh, advising him on matters of leadership, and assisting in conveying Allah's commands to the Israelites. Harun's loyalty, wisdom, and dedication were instrumental in the success of their mission.

Confrontation with the Pharaoh

Harun and Musa confronted the Pharaoh together, demanding the freedom of the Israelites and the cessation of their oppression. Harun's eloquence and persuasive abilities were evident during these encounters, as he conveyed Allah's message with clarity and conviction.

Leadership Among the Israelites

During Musa's absence when he received divine revelations, Harun assumed leadership among the Israelites. He guided them in matters of faith, upheld the teachings of Allah, and maintained unity and order within the community.

Construction of the Golden Calf Incident

One of the notable events involving Harun was the construction of the golden calf by some Israelites in Musa's absence. Despite his efforts to dissuade them from idol worship, Harun faced challenges in maintaining their faith. However, he remained steadfast in upholding monotheism and denounced the worship of idols.

Legacy and Lessons

Prophet Harun's story in Islamic tradition emphasizes the virtues of loyalty, support, and unity in faith. His role as a prophet and advisor to Musa highlights the importance of cooperation, leadership, and adherence to divine guidance.

Conclusion

Prophet Harun's life and contributions serve as a reminder of the essential qualities needed for effective leadership, guidance, and the preservation of faith. His unwavering support for Musa and commitment to Allah's commands exemplify the principles of devotion, wisdom, and steadfastness in the face of challenges.

17. The Story of Prophet Dawud (David)

Introduction

Prophet Dawud (David) is a revered figure in Islamic tradition, known for his wisdom, courage, piety, and leadership. His story, prominently mentioned in the Quran, includes his rise from shepherd to king, his struggles and triumphs, and his legacy as a righteous ruler and prophet.

Early Life and Calling

Prophet Dawud was born into the lineage of the Israelites during a time of turmoil and conflict. As a young shepherd, Dawud displayed exceptional bravery and devotion to Allah, which caught the attention of the people and eventually led to his prophethood.

Confrontation with Goliath

One of the most famous events in Dawud's life is his confrontation with the giant Goliath (Jalut). Despite his small stature, Dawud's unwavering faith in Allah and his skill with a sling enabled him to defeat Goliath and inspire awe and respect among the people.

Anointed as King

After the victory over Goliath, Dawud's reputation as a righteous and courageous individual grew, leading to his anointment as the king of Israel. Dawud's reign was marked by justice, compassion, and devotion to Allah's commands.

Dawud's Rule and Justice

As a king, Dawud ruled with fairness and wisdom, settling disputes among his people and upholding the teachings of Allah. He was known for his poetic and musical talents, composing Psalms that praised Allah and expressed his devotion.

The Story of Talut (Saul)

The Quran narrates the story of Talut (Saul), another king appointed by Allah to lead the Israelites alongside Prophet Dawud. Talut's selection as king was a test of the people's faith and loyalty, and Dawud played a crucial role in supporting and advising Talut during his reign.

Dawud's Repentance and Forgiveness

Prophet Dawud's story also includes moments of introspection and repentance. When he erred in judgment regarding the case of two disputing parties, Dawud realized his mistake and sought forgiveness from Allah. His sincere repentance and humility were met with Allah's forgiveness and mercy.

Legacy and Lessons

Prophet Dawud's life and rule serve as a timeless example of righteousness, humility, leadership, and devotion to Allah. His Psalms (Zabur) are revered as sacred scripture, providing guidance and inspiration to believers.

Conclusion

Prophet Dawud's story in Islamic tradition embodies the virtues of faith, courage, justice, and repentance. His legacy as a prophet, king, and poet continues to inspire believers to uphold righteousness, seek forgiveness, and remain steadfast in devotion to Allah.

18. The Story of Prophet Sulayman (Solomon)

Introduction

Prophet Sulayman (Solomon) is a significant and revered figure in Islamic tradition, known for his wisdom, justice, and miraculous abilities granted by Allah. His story, detailed in the Quran, portrays him as a powerful ruler, a devout worshiper, and a prophet with extraordinary gifts.

Early Life and Ascension to Kingship

Prophet Sulayman was the son of Prophet Dawud (David) and was chosen by Allah to succeed his father as the king of Israel. Despite his youth, Sulayman demonstrated exceptional wisdom and leadership qualities, which impressed his people and earned him the throne.

Wisdom and Judgment

One of the most famous accounts of Sulayman's wisdom is the story of the two disputing women who came to him for judgment regarding a child. Sulayman's ingenious solution, to discern the true mother by proposing to divide the child, revealed his exceptional wisdom and insight.

Kingdom and Rule

Under Sulayman's rule, the kingdom of Israel flourished. He governed with justice, fairness, and compassion, ensuring the well-being of his subjects and upholding Allah's laws. His kingdom was characterized by prosperity, harmony, and adherence to monotheism.

Miraculous Abilities

Prophet Sulayman was granted miraculous abilities by Allah, including the ability to communicate with animals and control the forces of nature. His command over the jinn (spirits) was particularly notable, as they aided him in various tasks and projects.

The Queen of Sheba

One of the notable events in Sulayman's life is his encounter with the Queen of Sheba (Bilqis). Impressed by Sulayman's reputation and wisdom, she visited his kingdom to test his knowledge and judgment. Sulayman's response to her challenges and questions further demonstrated his wisdom and insight.

Construction Projects and Innovations

Prophet Sulayman undertook significant construction projects during his reign, including the construction of the magnificent Temple of Solomon (Bait al-Maqdis), which served as a place of worship and a symbol of his devotion to Allah.

Psalms and Prayers

Sulayman's devotion to Allah is evident in his Psalms (Zabur) and prayers, which are mentioned in the Quran. His deep connection to Allah and his constant gratitude and supplication reflect his spiritual depth and sincerity.

Legacy and Lessons

Prophet Sulayman's story in Islamic tradition emphasizes the virtues of wisdom, justice, devotion, and humility. His legacy as a wise ruler, a devout worshiper, and a prophet with miraculous abilities continues to inspire believers to seek knowledge, uphold justice, and maintain a strong connection with Allah.

Conclusion

Prophet Sulayman's life and teachings serve as a timeless example of righteousness, wisdom, and devotion to Allah. His story highlights the importance of leadership with integrity, the pursuit of knowledge, and the recognition of Allah's blessings and guidance in all aspects of life.

19. The Story of Prophet Ilyas (Elias)

Introduction

Prophet Ilyas (Elias), known as Elijah in some traditions, is a revered figure in Islamic tradition, known for his unwavering faith, dedication to Allah, and his role as a reformer and preacher of monotheism. His story, mentioned in the Quran, highlights themes of resilience, trust in Allah, and the struggle against idolatry.

Early Life and Calling

Prophet Ilyas lived during a time when idol worship and polytheism were prevalent among his people. Despite the prevailing corruption and deviation from monotheism, Ilyas remained steadfast in his faith and devotion to Allah from a young age.

Mission and Confrontation with Idolatry

Ilyas was appointed by Allah as a prophet and tasked with calling his people to monotheism and the worship of Allah alone. He confronted the idolaters and urged them to abandon their false beliefs and practices, emphasizing the oneness of Allah and the futility of idol worship.

Miracle of the Rain

One of the notable events in Ilyas's life is the miracle of the rain, which occurred during a severe drought. In response to Ilyas's supplication and prayer, Allah sent rain to relieve the drought-stricken land, demonstrating divine intervention and the power of prophetic supplication.

Persecution and Trials

Despite his sincere efforts to guide his people, Ilyas faced opposition and persecution from the idolaters and corrupt leaders. He remained steadfast in his mission, enduring hardships and remaining faithful to Allah's commands.

Mount Carmel Contest

One of the dramatic events associated with Ilyas is the contest on Mount Carmel, where he challenged the idolaters and false prophets to a test of divine intervention. Through Allah's miraculous intervention, Ilyas's sacrifice was accepted, affirming the truth of his message and the power of monotheism.

Ascension and Legacy

Prophet Ilyas's story includes his miraculous ascension (Mi'raj) to the heavens, where he continued his mission and received divine revelations. His legacy as a fearless preacher of monotheism and a model of unwavering faith continues to inspire believers to uphold true belief and resist falsehood.

Lessons and Impact

The story of Prophet Ilyas in Islamic tradition serves as a reminder of the importance of steadfastness in faith, perseverance in the face of adversity, and trust in Allah's guidance. His struggle against idolatry and his unwavering commitment to monotheism exemplify the virtues of prophetic determination and devotion.

Conclusion

Prophet Ilyas's life and mission underscore the timeless principles of monotheism, faith, and divine intervention. His story inspires believers to stand firm in their beliefs, confront falsehood, and trust in Allah's wisdom and mercy.

20. The Story of Prophet Alyasa' (Elisha)

Introduction

Prophet Alyasa' (Elisha) is a revered figure in Islamic tradition, known for his prophethood, miracles, and dedication to spreading the message of monotheism. His story, though brief in Islamic sources compared to other prophets, carries profound lessons about faith, devotion, and divine intervention.

Early Life and Calling

Prophet Alyasa' lived during a time when idolatry and ignorance prevailed among his people. Despite the prevailing corruption, he remained steadfast in his belief in Allah and devoted himself to worship and obedience from a young age.

Appointment as Prophet

Alyasa' was appointed by Allah as a prophet and tasked with continuing the mission of his predecessor, Prophet Ilyas (Elijah). He carried forward the message of monotheism and guided his people away from idol worship and false beliefs.

Miraculous Abilities

Prophet Alyasa' was granted miraculous abilities by Allah, similar to his predecessor Ilyas. His miracles included healing the sick, reviving the dead, and providing sustenance in times of need, demonstrating the power of divine intervention and the authenticity of his prophethood.

The Widow's Oil and the Iron Axe

One of the notable miracles associated with Alyasa' is the story of the widow's oil and the iron axe. In one instance, Alyasa' helped a widow multiply her oil to pay off her debts, showcasing Allah's provision and abundance. In another instance, he retrieved a lost iron axe from the bottom of a river through divine intervention, further affirming his prophetic status.

Encounter with Kings and Rulers

Prophet Alyasa' interacted with kings and rulers during his prophetic mission, advising them on matters of faith, justice, and righteousness. His wisdom and guidance were sought after, and he fearlessly conveyed Allah's message without compromise.

Legacy and Impact

While the details of Alyasa''s life and mission are relatively limited in Islamic sources compared to other prophets, his story serves as a reminder of the power of faith, the reality of divine intervention, and the importance of adhering to monotheism and righteousness.

Lessons and Reflection

The story of Prophet Alyasa' encourages believers to trust in Allah's wisdom and mercy, to remain steadfast in faith despite challenges, and to seek guidance and inspiration from the lives of the prophets. His miracles and teachings exemplify the virtues of compassion, generosity, and devotion to Allah.

Conclusion

Prophet Alyasa''s story, although brief, carries timeless lessons about faith, miracles, and divine intervention. His dedication to spreading monotheism and righteousness continues to inspire believers to uphold true belief and strive for spiritual excellence.

21. The Story of Prophet Yunus (Jonah)

Introduction

The story of Prophet Yunus (Jonah) is a remarkable tale of repentance, mercy, and the power of Allah's guidance. It is narrated in both the Quran and Islamic tradition, teaching profound lessons about patience, humility, and the consequences of disobedience.

Early Life and Prophethood

Prophet Yunus was a righteous and devoted servant of Allah, chosen as a prophet to guide his people towards monotheism and righteousness. He preached tirelessly, calling his people to abandon their sinful ways and turn to Allah in repentance.

Reluctance and Departure

Despite Yunus's earnest efforts, his people persisted in their disobedience and disbelief. Feeling discouraged and disheartened by their rejection of his message, Yunus decided to leave his community without seeking Allah's guidance or permission.

The Incident with the Whale

As Yunus embarked on his journey, he boarded a ship that encountered a severe storm. Realizing that the storm was a consequence of his hasty departure and disobedience to Allah's command, Yunus acknowledged his mistake and voluntarily threw himself into the raging sea.

Swallowed by a Whale

Allah, in His infinite wisdom and mercy, commanded a great whale to swallow Yunus and protect him from drowning. Inside the belly of the whale, Yunus experienced solitude and reflection, realizing the gravity of his actions and seeking forgiveness from Allah with sincere repentance.

Prayer of Repentance

In the depths of darkness and despair, Yunus turned to Allah with a heartfelt prayer of repentance:

"There is no deity except You; exalted are You. Indeed, I have been of the wrongdoers." (Quran 21:87)

Mercy and Deliverance

Allah, in His boundless mercy, responded to Yunus's prayer and forgave him. He commanded the whale to release Yunus onto the shore, safe and unharmed. This miraculous deliverance served as a testament to Allah's compassion and willingness to forgive those who turn to Him in repentance.

Return to His People

After his ordeal, Yunus returned to his people with renewed determination and zeal. He continued his mission of calling them to repentance and monotheism, emphasizing the importance of humility, obedience, and reliance on Allah's mercy.

Lessons and Reflection

The story of Prophet Yunus teaches profound lessons about the consequences of disobedience, the power of sincere repentance, and the boundless mercy of Allah. It underscores the importance of patience, humility, and reliance on Allah's guidance in times of hardship and adversity.

Conclusion

Prophet Yunus's story serves as a timeless reminder of the transformative power of repentance and the depth of Allah's mercy. It inspires believers to seek forgiveness with sincerity, to learn from their mistakes, and to trust in Allah's wisdom and compassion.

22.The Story of Prophet Zakariya (Zechariah)

Introduction

Prophet Zakariya (Zechariah) is a revered figure in Islamic tradition, known for his piety, devotion, and the miraculous birth of his son, Yahya (John the Baptist). His story, detailed in the Quran, highlights the themes of faith, prayer, and the fulfillment of divine promises.

Early Life and Righteousness

Prophet Zakariya was a descendant of the Prophet Dawud (David) and served as a righteous and devout priest in the temple of Jerusalem. He dedicated his life to worshiping Allah and upholding the teachings of the Torah.

Prayer for Offspring

Despite his old age and his wife's infertility, Zakariya never lost hope in Allah's mercy. He fervently prayed for a righteous heir to continue his legacy and serve as a beacon of guidance for the people.

The Miracle of Yahya's Birth

Allah, in His infinite wisdom and power, answered Zakariya's prayers and bestowed upon him the glad tidings of a son, Yahya. This miraculous birth, given Zakariya's advanced age and his wife's barrenness, served as a testament to Allah's ability to fulfill His promises.

Yahya's Mission and Virtues

Yahya (John the Baptist) grew up to become a righteous prophet, preaching monotheism and calling people to repentance. He inherited his father's piety and devotion to Allah, embodying the virtues of humility, integrity, and dedication to divine guidance.

Zakariya's Role as a Mentor

Prophet Zakariya played a crucial role in nurturing Yahya's prophetic mission and spiritual development. He imparted wisdom, knowledge, and piety to his son, preparing him for the significant task of guiding the people towards righteousness.

The Table Spread (Ma'idah) Miracle

One of the miracles associated with Zakariya is the Table Spread (Ma'idah) miracle, where Allah provided a heavenly feast to confirm the truth of Zakariya's message and the authenticity of his prophethood.

Legacy and Impact

Prophet Zakariya's story in Islamic tradition emphasizes the importance of patience, steadfastness in faith, and the power of sincere supplication. His unwavering trust in Allah's mercy and the fulfillment of his prayers serve as an inspiration for believers to maintain hope and trust in Allah's divine plan.

Conclusion

Prophet Zakariya's life and the miraculous birth of Yahya highlight the transformative power of faith, prayer, and divine intervention. His story serves as a timeless example of devotion, perseverance, and the fulfillment of divine promises, encouraging believers to turn to Allah with trust and sincerity in times of need.

23.The Story of Prophet Yahya (John the Baptist)

Introduction

Prophet Yahya (John the Baptist) is a revered figure in Islamic tradition, known for his piety, asceticism, and role as a herald of the coming of Prophet Isa (Jesus). His story, mentioned in the Quran, highlights his righteous upbringing, prophetic mission, and martyrdom for the sake of truth.

Birth and Righteous Lineage

Yahya was born to Prophet Zakariya (Zechariah) and his wife, who were elderly and childless until Allah blessed them with Yahya as a result of Zakariya's supplications. Yahya's birth was miraculous and marked by divine favor.

Childhood and Upbringing

From a young age, Yahya displayed exceptional piety, wisdom, and devotion to Allah. He was raised in seclusion, away from worldly distractions, and devoted himself to prayer, fasting, and the study of divine scriptures.

Prophetic Mission

As Yahya reached adulthood, he was appointed as a prophet by Allah and entrusted with the mission of calling people to monotheism, righteousness, and repentance. He preached humility, honesty, and moral rectitude, urging his followers to purify their hearts and turn to Allah in devotion.

Preparing the Way for Prophet Isa

Yahya's prominent role was to prepare the way for the coming of Prophet Isa (Jesus). He foretold Isa's arrival and emphasized the importance of recognizing and following the true Messiah sent by Allah.

Baptism and Symbolism

One of the notable aspects of Yahya's mission was his practice of baptism (mubahalah), symbolizing purification and spiritual rebirth. Through baptism, Yahya invited people to repentance and renewal of faith, preparing them for the arrival of Prophet Isa.

Confrontation with Tyranny

Yahya fearlessly confronted the corrupt rulers and elites of his time, denouncing their injustice, arrogance, and immorality. His uncompromising stance for truth and righteousness earned him respect among the common people but also incurred the wrath of the oppressive authorities.

Martyrdom and Legacy

Yahya's unwavering commitment to truth and justice ultimately led to his martyrdom. He was imprisoned and eventually executed by the tyrannical ruler, Herod Antipas, for his uncompromising condemnation of Herod's immoral actions.

Divine Honor and Eternal Remembrance

Despite his tragic end, Prophet Yahya holds a revered status in Islamic tradition as a symbol of steadfastness, sacrifice, and unwavering devotion to Allah. His life and martyrdom serve as a reminder of the timeless struggle between truth and falsehood and the eternal reward awaiting those who remain steadfast in faith.

Conclusion

Prophet Yahya's story in Islamic tradition inspires believers to uphold righteousness, pursue spiritual purification, and remain steadfast in the face of adversity. His unwavering dedication to Allah's message and his role in preparing the way for Prophet Isa exemplify the virtues of prophetic commitment and the eternal significance of divine guidance.

24. The Story of Prophet Isa (Jesus)

Introduction

The story of Prophet Isa (Jesus) is one of the most significant and revered narratives in Islamic tradition, highlighting his miraculous birth, prophetic mission, teachings, and eventual ascension. Here is a comprehensive account of his life and impact:

Miraculous Birth

Prophet Isa's story begins with his miraculous birth to Maryam (Mary), a pious and devout woman chosen by Allah for this noble purpose. Isa's birth without a father is a testament to Allah's power and divine plan.

Prophetic Mission

As Isa grew, he was endowed with prophethood by Allah and tasked with calling people to monotheism, righteousness, and compassion. He performed numerous miracles from an early age, including speaking as an infant to defend his mother's honor.

Teachings and Miracles

Isa's teachings emphasized love, mercy, forgiveness, and the importance of spiritual purity. He performed extraordinary miracles, such as healing the sick, raising the dead, and providing sustenance miraculously, all by the permission of Allah.

Calling to Allah

Prophet Isa called people to worship Allah alone, rejecting idolatry, materialism, and hypocrisy. His message emphasized the inner dimensions of faith, emphasizing sincerity, humility, and devotion to Allah.

Opposition and Challenges

Despite his noble mission and miraculous abilities, Isa faced opposition from some factions, including religious leaders and those vested in worldly power. However, his steadfastness, wisdom, and compassion continued to draw followers who embraced his message of truth and righteousness.

The Last Supper and Crucifixion

The Last Supper, commemorated in Islamic tradition as a significant event in Isa's life, symbolized unity, humility, and sacrifice. However, the narrative of Isa's crucifixion diverges from Christian belief in Islam. Muslims believe that Isa was not crucified but was raised by Allah before any harm could come to him.

Return and Role in the End Times

Islamic belief holds that Prophet Isa will return to Earth in the end times as a just ruler and leader, establishing peace, justice, and the supremacy of Islam. His return signifies the culmination of divine justice and the fulfillment of prophetic prophecies.

Legacy and Impact

Prophet Isa's life and teachings have had a profound impact on millions of people around the world. His message of love, compassion, and devotion to Allah continues to inspire believers to strive for spiritual excellence and to embody the virtues of kindness, forgiveness, and humility.

Conclusion

Prophet Isa's story in Islamic tradition serves as a timeless reminder of the power of faith, compassion, and divine guidance. His life and teachings exemplify the ideals of prophet hood, steadfastness in truth, and the eternal mercy and wisdom of Allah.

25. The Story of Prophet Muhammad (PBUH)

Introduction

Prophet Muhammad, peace be upon him (PBUH), was born in Mecca in the year 570 CE, into the noble Quraysh tribe. His early life was marked by honesty, integrity, and a deep concern for the welfare of others, earning him the titles of Al-Amin (the Trustworthy) and As-Sadiq (the Truthful) among his people.

Early Life and Prophethood

Muhammad's upbringing was influenced by the prevailing pagan culture in Mecca. Despite this, he would often retreat to the cave of Hira for contemplation and worship, seeking spiritual guidance and solace.

At the age of 40, while meditating in the cave, Muhammad received his first revelation from Allah through the Angel Gabriel. This event marked the beginning of his prophethood and the revelation of the Quran, the holy book of Islam.

Spreading the Message

Initially, Muhammad preached the message of Islam privately to his close family and friends, gradually expanding his circle of followers. His teachings emphasized the Oneness of Allah (Tawhid), social justice, compassion, and moral integrity.

Despite facing opposition and persecution from the Quraysh tribe and other adversaries, Muhammad remained steadfast in his mission, calling people to worship Allah alone and to uphold righteous conduct.

Migration to Medina (Hijrah)

As persecution in Mecca intensified, Muhammad and his followers faced increasing hostility and threats to their safety. In 622 CE, they migrated to the city of Yathrib, later known as Medina, marking the beginning of the Islamic lunar calendar and the establishment of the first Muslim community.

Consolidation of the Community

In Medina, Muhammad played a pivotal role in uniting the diverse tribes and communities under the banner of Islam. He established a constitution (the Constitution of Medina) that guaranteed rights and protections for all residents, regardless of their faith or background.

Muhammad's leadership in Medina encompassed social, political, and spiritual dimensions. He implemented reforms, resolved disputes, and laid the foundations for a just and compassionate society based on Islamic principles.

Challenges and Victories

During his prophethood, Muhammad faced numerous challenges, including armed conflicts with adversaries who sought to extinguish Islam. Despite these challenges, Muhammad's leadership, strategic acumen, and unwavering faith led to significant victories, including the peaceful conquest of Mecca in 630 CE.

Final Years and Legacy

In the final years of his life, Muhammad continued to guide and teach his followers, emphasizing the importance of piety, humility, and adherence to the teachings of Islam. He performed the Farewell Pilgrimage (Hajj) in 632 CE, delivering his famous sermon known as the Farewell Sermon, which encapsulated key principles of Islam and emphasized unity, equality, and justice.

Prophet Muhammad passed away in Medina in 632 CE, leaving behind a legacy of prophethood, exemplary character, and divine guidance encapsulated in the Quran. His teachings continue to inspire millions of Muslims worldwide, guiding them on the path of righteousness, compassion, and devotion to Allah.

About the Author

Arief Muinnudin was born in Malaysia in 1987, where he discovered his passion for writing at a young age. Growing up surrounded by the diverse cultures and vibrant landscapes of Malaysia, Arief developed a deep appreciation for storytelling and the power of words to connect people from different backgrounds.

From his early years, Arief was drawn to literature and the art of crafting narratives that captivate and inspire readers. He immersed himself in a wide range of genres, from fiction to non-fiction, exploring various themes and styles to hone his writing skills.

As Arief's love for writing blossomed, so did his ambition to share meaningful stories with the world. He embarked on a journey to become a published author, dedicating countless hours to researching, writing, and refining his manuscripts.

With each book he wrote, Arief aimed to engage readers on a profound level, sparking discussions, provoking thought, and leaving a lasting impact on their lives. His commitment to creating compelling and insightful content earned him recognition as a talented writer with a unique voice and perspective.

Arief's passion for literature continues to drive him forward, inspiring him to explore new ideas, tackle challenging topics, and connect with readers on a deeper level through the power of storytelling.

Read more at https://ariefebook.etsy.com.